for Advent

SACRED SPACE

for Advent and the Christmas Season 2016–17

SACRED SPACE

November 27, 2016, to January 8, 2017

from the website www.sacredspace.ie

Prayer from the Irish Jesuits

LOYOLA PRESS.
A JESUIT MINISTRY
Chicago

LOYOLA PRESS.
A JESUIT MINISTRY

3441 N. Ashland Avenue
Chicago, Illinois 60657
(800) 621-1008
www.loyolapress.com

Scripture quotations are from *New Revised Standard Version Bible: Catholic Edition*, copyright © 1989, 1993 National Council of the Churches of Christ in the United States of America. Used by permission. All rights reserved.

Advent retreat by Fr. Michael Paul Gallagher, SJ, used with permission.

Cover art credit: © iStock/Qweek

ISBN-13: 978-0-8294-4446-9
ISBN-10: 0-8294-4446-7

16 17 18 19 20 Versa 10 9 8 7 6 5 4 3 2 1

Contents

The Presence of God

Bless all who worship you, almighty God,
from the rising of the sun to its setting:
from your goodness enrich us,
by your love inspire us,
by your Spirit guide us,
by your power protect us,
in your mercy receive us,
now and always.

How to Use This Booklet

During each week of Advent, begin by reading the "Something to think and pray about each day this week." Then go through "The Presence of God," "Freedom," and "Consciousness" steps to help you prepare yourself to hear the Word of God speaking to you. In the next step, "The Word," turn to the Scripture reading for each day of the week. Inspiration points are provided if you need them. Then return to the "Conversation" and "Conclusion" steps. Follow this process every day of Advent.

The Advent retreat at the back of this book follows a similar structure: an invitation to experience still-ness, a Scripture passage and reflection points, and suggestions for prayer; you may find it useful to move back and forth between the daily reflections and the retreat.

November 27—December 3, 2016

Something to think and pray about each day this week:

The Dynamic of Hope

A driving dynamic of Advent is hope. If we had nothing to hope for, there would be no point to this season. The original hope was for a child to be born who would bring justice and peace to the world and who would heal the rift between humanity and God. But that larger hope is filled with smaller ones—daily hopes that can shape us as people. Some hopes will shape our relationships. The Christ Child grew to be a man who embodied forgiveness and generosity. A life of hope sees the good in others, is patient with their shortcomings, and tenaciously envisions them at their best. Some hopes will shape our life work. The promised Messiah proclaimed God's realm of justice and mercy. No matter what jobs we do or work positions we hold, as hopeful people we maintain fairness and integrity as short-term and long-term goals. We make our work matter for the common good. Some hopes will shape our character. Jesus exemplified hope that cultivates true interior freedom. A hopeful person cannot continue in anxiety, grasping, need for

control, and habitual anger. How is hope visible in
your life? Where has it faded?
                        —Vinita Hampton Wright, Loyola Press blogs

The Presence of God

Be still and know that I am God. Lord, may your
spirit guide me to seek your loving presence more and
more. For it is there I find rest and refreshment from
this busy world.

Freedom

By God's grace I was born to live in freedom. Free
to enjoy the pleasures He created for me. Dear Lord,
grant that I may live as you intended, with complete
confidence in your loving care.

Consciousness

In God's loving presence I unwind the past day,
starting from now and looking back, moment by
moment.
I gather in all the goodness and light, in gratitude.
I attend to the shadows and what they say to me,
seeking healing, courage, forgiveness.

The Word

The Word of God comes to us through the Scriptures.
May the Holy Spirit enlighten my mind and heart to
respond to the gospel teachings. (Please turn to the

Scriptures on the following pages. Inspiration points are there should you need them. When you are ready, return here to continue.)

Conversation
Jesus, you always welcomed little children when you walked on this earth. Teach me to have a childlike trust in you. To live in the knowledge that you will never abandon me.

Conclusion
Glory be to the Father, and to the Son, and to the Holy Spirit,
As it was in the beginning, is now and ever shall be,
World without end. Amen.

Sunday 27th November
First Sunday of Advent
Matthew 24:37–44

For as the days of Noah were, so will be the coming of the Son of Man. For as in those days before the flood they were eating and drinking, marrying and giving in marriage, until the day Noah entered the ark, and they knew nothing until the flood came and swept them all away, so too will be the coming of the Son of Man. Then two will be in the field; one will be taken and one will be left. Two women will be grinding meal together; one will be taken and one will be left. Keep awake therefore, for you do not know on what day your Lord is coming. But understand this: if the owner of the house had known in what part of the night the thief was coming, he would have stayed awake and would not have let his house be broken into. Therefore you also must be ready, for the Son of Man is coming at an unexpected hour.

- There are tough images here: floods, capture, thieving. These are frightening, life-changing events. We have one life, and it is precious and fragile. We need to be in tune with Jesus constantly, ready for whatever comes our way, not sleep-walking through life.

- Lord, make me present to your daily appearances in my life. As the poet Tagore says: "He comes,

comes, ever comes." Lord, do not let me miss you, even in my ordinary routine.

Monday 28th November
Matthew 8:5–11

When Jesus entered Capernaum, a centurion came to him, appealing to him and saying, "Lord, my servant is lying at home paralyzed, in terrible distress." And he said to him, "I will come and cure him." The centurion answered, "Lord, I am not worthy to have you come under my roof; but only speak the word, and my servant will be healed. For I also am a man under authority, with soldiers under me; and I say to one, 'Go,' and he goes, and to another, 'Come,' and he comes, and to my slave, 'Do this,' and the slave does it." When Jesus heard him, he was amazed and said to those who followed him, "Truly I tell you, in no one in Israel have I found such faith. I tell you, many will come from east and west and will eat with Abraham and Isaac and Jacob in the kingdom of heaven."

- The centurion was an officer of the imperial army, a man with power and status. He was begging a favor from a penniless itinerant teacher and declaring himself unworthy even to entertain Jesus in his house. Jesus was amazed, not merely at the trust of the man, but at the fact that his love for his servant led him to cut through all the barriers of rank and race. Lord, so much of my life is structured by social conventions and barriers. Give me the grace to listen to my heart and reach out to those that I can help.

- This miracle is unusual for two reasons. Jesus was not actually present when the healing took place: he spoke the word, and the centurion's servant was healed. The servant did not even have to hear Jesus speak the word: it was enough that the word was spoken. Do we realize that when we speak God's word, someone, somewhere, may find healing?

Tuesday 29th November
Luke 10:21–24

Jesus rejoiced in the Holy Spirit and said, "I thank you, Father, Lord of heaven and earth, because you have hidden these things from the wise and the intelligent and have revealed them to infants; yes, Father, for such was your gracious will. All things have been handed over to me by my Father; and no one knows who the Son is except the Father, or who the Father is except the Son and anyone to whom the Son chooses to reveal him." Then turning to the disciples, Jesus said to them privately, "Blessed are the eyes that see what you see! For I tell you that many prophets and kings desired to see what you see, but did not see it, and to hear what you hear, but did not hear it."

- In this scene, Jesus seems to be rejoicing in his disciples, happy that they are with him. He is happy, too, in what God his Father has given to his followers. Jesus rejoices in us just as friends rejoice together and as parents rejoice in the talents and gifts of their children. Perhaps, then, can we rejoice in one another? In prayer we can allow ourselves to be grateful for the goodness, gifts, and faith of others, especially people who are significant in our lives.

- I watch Jesus at his prayer. What is it like to see him rejoicing in the Holy Spirit and thanking his Father? At this moment as I pray, the three divine Persons are present with me, and the Spirit is praying in me. Awareness of this can transform my prayer.

Wednesday 30th November
Matthew 4:18–22

As Jesus walked by the Sea of Galilee, he saw two brothers, Simon, who is called Peter, and Andrew his brother, casting a net into the sea—for they were fishermen. And he said to them, "Follow me, and I will make you fish for people." Immediately they left their nets and followed him. As he went from there, he saw two other brothers, James son of Zebedee and his brother John, in the boat with their father Zebedee, mending their nets, and he called them. Immediately they left the boat and their father, and followed him.

- Jesus called the fishermen, speaking to them in terms they recognized. Jesus calls me as I am, wanting me to use my skills and abilities to draw others to life. Peter, Andrew, James, and John responded to Jesus immediately. I think of how slow my reactions are. I try to see what holds me back, and I talk to Jesus about it.

- In the middle of any ordinary day Jesus walks by, sees me, singles me out from the crowd, speaks to me, and invites my discipleship. What attracts me to Jesus? What helps me respond generously to him? Am I a close follower of his, or do I keep my eye on him only occasionally?

Thursday 1st December
Matthew 7:21, 24–27

Jesus said to the people, "Not everyone who says to me, 'Lord, Lord,' will enter the kingdom of heaven, but only the one who does the will of my Father in heaven. Everyone then who hears these words of mine and acts on them will be like a wise man who built his house on rock. The rain fell, the floods came, and the winds blew and beat on that house, but it did not fall, because it had been founded on rock. And everyone who hears these words of mine and does not act on them will be like a foolish man who built his house on sand. The rain fell, and the floods came, and the winds blew and beat against that house, and it fell—and great was its fall!"

- Saint Ignatius remarks that love is found in deeds rather than in words. Jesus praises good deeds over good intentions that are not carried out. I pray to be like a good servant who does the work God invites me to do.

- Hearing or reading God's Word is important, but it is not the end. I take time to let the Word of God settle into the shape of my life. I take care not to let it merely stay in my mind but to let it touch my heart and desires as well. I ask God to help me be present to the Word. My words are part of my response to God, but I realize that it is not just the saying of words that is important. I ask for sincerity and integrity, that my words will become actions that become my way of life.

Friday 2nd December
Matthew 9:27–31

As Jesus went on his way, two blind men followed him, crying loudly, "Have mercy on us, Son of David!" When he entered the house, the blind men came to him; and Jesus said to them, "Do you believe that I am able to do this?" They said to him,

"Yes, Lord." Then he touched their eyes and said, "According to your faith let it be done to you." And their eyes were opened. Then Jesus sternly ordered them, "See that no one knows of this." But they went away and spread the news about him throughout that district.

- How could these men follow Jesus if they could not see? By hearing his voice, perhaps. Or maybe others led them to him. How did they know what to ask for? They knew they needed physical *and* spiritual sight, so they asked for more than sight: they asked for mercy. Their faith in Jesus opened their hearts to appeal to him. Their faith touched power in Jesus, and they were healed. They knew their need for God and for others; they did not hide their need and thus were healed.

- Lord, you do not meet me as one of a multitude, but face to face, on my own, where you can test the truth of my words. You meet me and listen to my desire when it is free from the illusions of mass emotion.

Saturday 3rd December
Matthew 9:35–10:1, 5a, 6–8

Jesus went about all the cities and villages, teaching in their synagogues, and proclaiming the good news of the kingdom, and curing every disease and every sickness. When he saw the crowds, he had compassion for them, because they were harassed and helpless, like sheep without a shepherd. Then he said to his disciples, "The harvest is plentiful, but the laborers are few; therefore ask the Lord of the harvest to send out laborers into his harvest." Then Jesus summoned his twelve disciples and gave them authority over unclean spirits, to cast them out, and to cure every disease and every sickness. These twelve Jesus sent out with the following instructions: "Go to the lost sheep of the house of Israel. As you go, proclaim the good news, 'The kingdom of heaven has come near.' Cure the sick, raise the dead, cleanse the lepers, cast out demons. You received without payment; give without payment."

- This seems to be a really outgoing Gospel reading: we are to look at the big harvest—the sick, the dead, the outcasts. All the needs of people are part of prayer. It is in care and compassion that the kingdom of heaven comes near.

- Lord, the cries of the poor and brokenhearted are evident in the mass migrations daily beamed into my living room. Let me not forget that you summon me today to be your eyes, your ears, and your hands of compassion. May I respond with loving compassion to all who come to me.

December 4—December 10, 2016

Something to think and pray about each day this week:

God's Big Dreams for Us

Over time, I've come to believe that God and God's people are certainly trying their best to make my life a glorious adventure. Some of the biggest life changes I've experienced were not initiated by me, but by my superiors and/or by circumstances. At those moments, I've often found it difficult to see where God is involved, but once I get settled into my new situation and gain a little perspective, I begin to see and appreciate that the move was good and the change was needed for me to stretch and grow. God works through others and through me to lead me to a fuller and better life. I believe that God has big dreams for all of us and is constantly inviting us to choose freedom over fear, generosity over greed, compassion over comparison, and service over selfishness. As such, I'm sure that God is involved in all our decisions, no matter how seemingly trivial. But I'm also sure that God is there plotting to make me happy, so God is not there with a divine remote control but, instead, gently invites us to greater love.

—Paul Brian Campbell, SJ, Loyola Press blogs

The Presence of God

I pause for a moment and think of the love and the grace that God showers on me: I am created in the image and likeness of God; I am God's dwelling place.

Freedom

Lord, you created me to live in freedom. May your Holy Spirit guide me to follow you freely. Instill in my heart a desire to know and love you more each day.

Consciousness

How am I really feeling? Lighthearted? Heavy hearted? I may be very much at peace, happy to be here. Equally, I may be frustrated, worried, or angry.
I acknowledge how I really am. It is the real me that the Lord loves.

The Word

I read the Word of God slowly, a few times over, and I listen to what God is saying to me. (Please turn to the Scripture on the following pages. Inspiration points are there should you need them. When you are ready, return here to continue.)

Conversation

I know with certainty there were times when you carried me, Lord. When it was through your strength I got through the dark times in my life.

Conclusion

I thank God for these moments we have spent together and for any insights I may have been given concerning the text.

Sunday 4th December
Second Sunday of Advent

Matthew 3:1–12

In those days John the Baptist appeared in the wilderness of Judea, proclaiming, "Repent, for the kingdom of heaven has come near." This is the one of whom the prophet Isaiah spoke when he said, "The voice of one crying out in the wilderness: 'Prepare the way of the Lord, make his paths straight.'" Now John wore clothing of camel's hair with a leather belt around his waist, and his food was locusts and wild honey. Then the people of Jerusalem and all Judea were going out to him, and all the region along the Jordan, and they were baptized by him in the river Jordan, confessing their sins. But when he saw many Pharisees and Sadducees coming for baptism, he said to them, "You brood of vipers! Who warned you to flee from the wrath to come? Bear fruit worthy of repentance. Do not presume to say to yourselves, 'We have Abraham as our ancestor'; for I tell you, God is able from these stones to raise up children to Abraham. Even now the axe is lying at the root of the trees; every tree therefore that does not bear good fruit is cut down and thrown into the fire. I baptize you with water for repentance, but one who is more powerful than I is coming after me; I am not worthy to carry his sandals. He will baptize you with the Holy Spirit and fire. His winnowing fork is in his hand, and he will clear his threshing floor and will gather his wheat into the granary; but the chaff he will burn with unquenchable fire."

- I may feel uncomfortable when confronted with John's call to repentance, but I let myself listen, acknowledging that I am a sinner in need of God's mercy. If I cannot admit this, then perhaps Advent is not for me.

- God does not want me to receive the Word passively. I work *with* God, preparing the way in my life, expectant and hopefully watching for God's approach.

Monday 5th December
Luke 5:17–26

One day, while Jesus was teaching, Pharisees and teachers of the law were sitting nearby (they had come from every village of Galilee and Judea and from Jerusalem); and the power of the Lord was with him to heal. Just then some men came, carrying a paralyzed man on a bed. They were trying to bring him in and lay him before Jesus; but finding no way to bring him in because of the crowd, they went up on the roof and let him down with his bed through the tiles into the middle of the crowd in front of Jesus. When he saw their faith, he said, "Friend, your sins are forgiven you." Then the scribes and Pharisees began to ask themselves, "Who is this who is speaking blasphemies? Who can forgive sins but God alone?" When Jesus perceived their questionings, he answered them, "Why do you raise such questions in your hearts? Which is easier, to say, 'Your sins are forgiven,' or to say, 'Stand up and walk'? But so that you may know that the Son of Man has authority on earth to forgive sins"—he said to the man who was paralyzed—"I say to you, stand up and take your bed and go to your home." Immediately he stood up before them, picked up what he had been lying on, and went home, glorifying God. Amazement seized all of them, and they glorified God and were filled with awe, saying, "We have seen strange things today."

- What an interesting, colorful, humorous, and yet life-changing scene! The man's friends are not easily put off. They use team effort and creativity to ensure that their paralyzed friend meets Jesus. An encounter happens that heals his body but also frees him from the paralysis of sin. Lord, forgiveness is a pressing need for all. Help me to do all I can to bring people to meet you and know your healing forgiveness in their lives. But help me do it sensitively!

- In this miracle, Jesus performs both a spiritual and a physical healing. Am I a spiritual paralytic? What might be crippling me in following Jesus?

Tuesday 6th December
Matthew 18:12–14

Jesus said, "What do you think? If a shepherd has a hundred sheep, and one of them has gone astray, does he not leave the ninety–nine on the mountains and go in search of the one that went astray? And if he finds it, truly I tell you, he rejoices over it more than over the ninety–nine that never went astray. So it is not the will of your Father in heaven that one of these little ones should be lost."

- Every Gospel passage tells us something about God. Here I learn that God has a particular care for everyone, especially for those who have gone astray. This is a comfort to me because I often lose my way in life. God is watching out for me always.

- I ask the Lord that I, too, may care for the "little ones"—those who are vulnerable and cannot cope with life's demands.

Wednesday 7th December
Matthew 11:28–30

Jesus said, "Come to me, all you that are weary and are carrying heavy burdens, and I will give you rest. Take my yoke upon you, and learn from me; for I am gentle and humble in heart, and you will find rest for your souls. For my yoke is easy, and my burden is light."

- Jesus invites us to come to him just as we are. He recognizes the busyness of our lives, how we labor and are overburdened, and he draws us into his loving and gentle presence. He wants to listen to all our troubles, and he assures us that his yoke is easy and his burden is light. When we spend time with Jesus, we find rest for our souls. He speaks to us in the silence of our hearts and gives us inner peace.

- Sometimes we carry heavy burdens because we want to figure things out on our own, believing there is no one to help us. I pray that people who are weighed down may hear the voice of Jesus. I pray that I may hear it, too, and have the humility I need to ask for and receive help.

Thursday 8th December
The Immaculate Conception
of the Blessed Virgin Mary
Luke 1:26–38

In the sixth month the angel Gabriel was sent by God to a town in Galilee called Nazareth, to a virgin engaged to a man whose name was Joseph, of the house of David. The virgin's name was Mary. And he came to her and said, "Greetings, favored one! The Lord is with you." But she was much perplexed by his words and pondered what sort of greeting this might be.

The angel said to her, "Do not be afraid, Mary, for you have found favor with God. And now, you will conceive in your womb and bear a son, and you will name him Jesus. He will be great, and will be called the Son of the Most High, and the Lord God will give to him the throne of his ancestor David. He will reign over the house of Jacob forever, and of his kingdom there will be no end." Mary said to the angel, "How can this be, since I am a virgin?" The angel said to her, "The Holy Spirit will come upon you, and the power of the Most High will overshadow you; therefore the child to be born will be holy; he will be called Son of God. And now, your relative Elizabeth in her old age has also conceived a son; and this is the sixth month for her who was said to be barren. For nothing will be impossible with God." Then Mary said, "Here am I, the servant of the Lord; let it be with me according to your word." Then the angel departed from her.

- Like Mary, I came into the world for a purpose. That purpose probably will not be revealed to me as dramatically as it was to her. Perhaps she heard God's message so clearly because she was comfortable with silence. Too often I fear the emptiness, the darkness, the silence within me. Yet it is there that the Spirit lives and works, even when my prayer seems most arid. God, help me go daily into the quiet of my heart, to meet you there, in love and adoration.

- Mary did not receive the angel's message as a total surprise; she was ready to engage in conversation with God's messenger. I turn to God in my prayer and try to see God's finger at work in my life. I draw inspiration from Mary's disposition.

Friday 9th December
Matthew 11:16–19

Jesus spoke to the crowds, "But to what will I compare this generation? It is like children sitting in the marketplaces and calling to one another, 'We played the flute for you, and you did not dance; we wailed, and you did not mourn.' For John came neither eating nor drinking, and they say, 'He has a demon'; the Son of Man came eating and drinking, and they say, 'Look, a glutton and a drunkard, a friend of tax collectors and sinners!' Yet wisdom is vindicated by her deeds."

- Both John and Jesus reveal what God is like, but they are misunderstood and cruelly rejected. I thank Jesus that he does not despair of humankind. He knows what we are like, yet he also sees what we can become. May I never despair over myself or others.

- How much am I willing to put myself out for others, as John and Jesus did? I pray not to be imprisoned in my comfort zones.

Saturday 10th December
Matthew 17:9a, 10–13

The disciples asked Jesus, "Why, then, do the scribes say that Elijah must come first?" He replied, "Elijah is indeed coming and will restore all things; but I tell you that Elijah has already come, and they did not recognize him, but they did to him whatever they pleased. So also the Son of Man is about to suffer at their hands." Then the disciples understood that he was speaking to them about John the Baptist.

- The disciples are bewildered. They believe that Elijah must return before the reign of God comes about. Jesus tries to move them on by telling them that the work of Elijah has already been done by John the Baptist. God moves at a pace that is different from ours. Do I also get stuck and miss the God of Surprises?

- What is preventing me from living as if my savior—my Redeemer—has already come? The philosopher Nietzsche remarked that Jesus' disciples "should look a little more redeemed"!

December 11—December 17, 2016

Something to think and pray about each day this week:

Preparing Our Hearts

"Are you ready for Christmas?" asked a guy I see at the train station every day. I thought of the long list of gifts I still needed to buy and the calendar crammed with holiday events and parties, and I shook my head. "Hardly," I said, and we both laughed knowingly. On my train ride downtown I turned off my iPod and let my mind ponder that question a little deeper. "Am I ready for Christmas?" This time I thought about the meaning of the holiday—the Son of God coming to earth to dwell among us and show us the way to eternal life. Again I shook my head and murmured to myself, "Hardly." It was then that I vowed to take advantage of every opportunity to prepare my heart for the coming of the Christ Child into the world—the world you and I live in. What I discovered was that if we know what we're preparing for, everything we encounter on the way to Christmas can prepare us for the coming of Christ, not only in Bethlehem 2,000 years ago but also in our homes, our families, our workplaces, and our communities. The usual December distractions can instead become holy moments when we find the Christ Child in our midst. Having the right attitude and perspective on the season will help you and your family avoid the excesses that make certain Christmas preparations frantic, yet draining and disappointing. As theologian John Shea says, "The task seems to be the delicate one of learning to make the customs and traditions of Christmas serve the Spirit."

—Tom McGrath, Loyola Press blogs

The Presence of God

Jesus, help me to be fully alive to your Holy Presence. Enfold me in your love. Let my heart become one with yours.

Freedom

I will ask God's help,
to be free from my own preoccupations,
to be open to God in this time of prayer,
to come to know, love, and serve God more.

Consciousness

I ask how I am within myself today. Am I particularly tired, stressed, or off form? If any of these characteristics apply, can I try to let go of the concerns that disturb me?

The Word
God speaks to each of us individually. I listen attentively to hear what God is saying to me. Read the text a few times, then listen. (Please turn to the Scripture on the following pages. Inspiration points are there should you need them. When you are ready, return here to continue.)

Conversation
Sometimes I wonder what I might say if I were to meet you in person, Lord.
I think I might say, "Thank you, Lord" for always being there for me.

Conclusion
Glory be to the Father, and to the Son, and to the Holy Spirit,
As it was in the beginning, is now and ever shall be,
World without end. Amen.

Sunday 11th December
Third Sunday of Advent

Matthew 11:2–11

When John heard in prison what the Messiah was doing, he sent word by his disciples and said to him, "Are you the one who is to come, or are we to wait for another?" Jesus answered them, "Go and tell John what you hear and see: the blind receive their sight, the lame walk, the lepers are cleansed, the deaf hear, the dead are raised, and the poor have good news brought to them. And blessed is anyone who takes no offence at me." As they went away, Jesus began to speak to the crowds about John: "What did you go out into the wilderness to look at? A reed shaken by the wind? What then did you go out to see? Someone dressed in soft robes? Look, those who wear soft robes are in royal palaces. What then did you go out to see? A prophet? Yes, I tell you, and more than a prophet. This is the one about whom it is written, 'See, I am sending my messenger ahead of you, who will prepare your way before you.' Truly I tell you, among those born of women no one has arisen greater than John the Baptist; yet the least in the kingdom of heaven is greater than he."

- There is real comfort in this story. John the Baptist, the powerful, austere man who held such a sway among the Jews, still had his moments of darkness. Imprisoned in Herod's dungeon, he wondered: *Am I a fool? Is this all there is? Was I wrong about Jesus?* He does not just brood on the question; he sends messengers to Jesus. And Jesus does not send back reassurances; rather, he asks the messengers to open their eyes and see the evidence of Jesus' life.

- "Go and tell what you hear and see . . . the blind receive their sight . . ."! What do I see and hear? Do I see the signs of God's kingdom breaking through in the world around me? What does it look like? If I don't see any positive signs, why not? Do I need to look again, or look differently? Am I somehow looking for "soft robes and royal palaces" when God is offering me a prophet?

Monday 12th December
Luke 1:26–38

In the sixth month the angel Gabriel was sent by God to a town in Galilee called Nazareth, to a virgin engaged to a man whose name was Joseph, of the house of David. The virgin's name was Mary. And he came to her and said, "Greetings, favored one! The Lord is with you." But she was much perplexed by his words and pondered what sort of greeting this might be. The angel said to her, "Do not be afraid, Mary, for you have found favor with God. And now, you will conceive in your womb and bear a son, and you will name him Jesus. He will be great, and will be called the Son of the Most High, and the Lord God will give to him the throne of his ancestor David. He will reign over the house of Jacob forever, and of his kingdom there will be no end." Mary said to the angel, "How can this be, since I am a virgin?" The angel said to her, "The Holy Spirit will come upon you, and the power of the Most High will overshadow you; therefore the child to be born will be holy; he will be called Son of God. And now, your relative Elizabeth in her old age has also conceived a son; and this is the sixth month for her who was said to be barren. For nothing will be impossible with God." Then Mary said, "Here am I, the servant of the Lord; let it be with me according to your word." Then the angel departed from her.

- Gabriel's message is condensed, intense, and direct. Mary is told that God favors her. She is to become pregnant by the Holy Spirit. She is to be the mother of the long-awaited Messiah. Her aged relative is already expecting a son. Each part of this sequence requires deep reflection, and yet we have the wonder of Mary's immediate consent. What might have prepared her to hear such a message?

- "Let it be with me according to your word." We remember Mary's words whenever we pray the

Angelus. Lord, this is not an easy prayer to make. You prayed it yourself in Gethsemane in a sweat of blood: "Not my will but yours be done." Help me make this prayer the pattern of my life. What issues of surrender and trust does it raise for me?

Tuesday 13th December
Matthew 21:28–32

Jesus said, "What do you think? A man had two sons; he went to the first and said, 'Son, go and work in the vineyard today.' He answered, 'I will not'; but later he changed his mind and went. The father went to the second and said the same; and he answered, 'I go, sir'; but he did not go. Which of the two did the will of his father?" They said, "The first." Jesus said to them, "Truly I tell you, the tax collectors and the prostitutes are going into the kingdom of God ahead of you. For John came to you in the way of righteousness and you did not believe him, but the tax collectors and the prostitutes believed him; and even after you saw it, you did not change your minds and believe him."

• Well, which person am I? The smooth but unreliable daddy-pleaser or the guy who, even with a bad attitude, does the job? The kingdom of heaven is not promised to the charmers but to those whose lives would make no sense if God did not exist.

- I review the statements and declarations I may have made. I ask God to help me abide by them and to help me accept forgiveness for wherever I have fallen short. God continually invites me to fullness of life. I do not have to be downhearted because I'm aware that I don't always accept the invitation. Rather, I can be encouraged that God puts trust in me by calling me to serve others.

Wednesday 14th December
Luke 7:18b–23

At that time, John summoned two of his disciples and sent them to the Lord to ask, "Are you the one who is to come, or are we to wait for another?" When the men had come to him, they said, "John the Baptist has sent us to you to ask, 'Are you the one who is to come, or are we to wait for another?'" Jesus had just then cured many people of diseases, plagues, and evil spirits, and had given sight to many who were blind. And he answered them, "Go and tell John what you have seen and heard: the blind receive their sight, the lame walk, the lepers are cleansed, the deaf hear, the dead are raised, the poor have good news brought to them. And blessed is anyone who takes no offence at me."

- The Jews wanted a political Messiah who would dramatically terminate their oppression under Roman rule. But Jesus' good news was not about war or politics. His message was meant especially for the blind, the lame, the lepers, the deaf, the dead, and the poor. I ask Jesus for the wisdom to avoid getting lost in political issues. I pray for the grace to share my love with those who are marginalized and unwanted by the world.

• John has been tossed into prison. As he languishes there, the oil of John's lamp is flickering. He wonders, did he get it right? Was his ministry a waste? Was Jesus the one he believed him to be? Lord, I can identify with John. I find that the wick of my lamp can quiver and splutter when things don't go my way. My desire for a world of peace and justice is met by a world of violence and injustice. This Advent day, refill my inner lamp and let me walk in faith and trust.

Thursday 15th December
Luke 7:24–30

When John's messengers had gone, Jesus began to speak to the crowds about John: "What did you go out into the wilderness to look at? A reed shaken by the wind? What then did you go out to see? Someone dressed in soft robes? Look, those who put on fine clothing and live in luxury are in royal palaces. What then did you go out to see? A prophet? Yes, I tell you, and more than a prophet. This is the one about whom it is written, 'See, I am sending my messenger ahead of you, who will prepare your way before you.' I tell you, among those born of women no one is greater than John; yet the least in the kingdom of God is greater than he." (And all the people who heard this, including the tax collectors, acknowledged the justice of God, because they had been baptized with John's baptism. But by refusing to be baptized by him, the Pharisees and the lawyers rejected God's purpose for themselves.)

- What do I go out to see? What are my true values? What impresses me? Jesus was impressed by John because he expressed God's values and chose simplicity of life. I ask him if he is impressed by me, and I listen in my heart to what he says to me.

- Luke uses a Hebrew poetic form of speaking—with repetition, question, and answer—to emphasize that with Jesus' ministry a new world order is beginning. I thank Jesus that I know the divine project, which John could not have known. I ask that I may help in the unfolding of God's intentions for the world. I can be at least a very minor prophet by living the gospel in my place and time.

Friday 16th December
John 5:33–36

Jesus said, "You sent messengers to John, and he testified to the truth. Not that I accept such human testimony, but I say these things so that you may be saved. He was a burning and shining lamp, and you were willing to rejoice for a while in his light. But I have a testimony greater than John's. The works that the Father has given me to complete, the very works that I am doing, testify on my behalf that the Father has sent me."

- Jesus points out that John's message was indeed a light to the people but that now there is a brighter light, which is Jesus. Sometimes we must transition from one wisdom or enlightenment to another. When do we know it's time to do this? Am I comfortable with the idea that I might need to make such a shift in my spiritual attention?

- What "works" are evidence that God is present? Many people claim to do God's works and deliver God's message, but certainly not all of them speak the truth. Holy Spirit, help me discern when what I am witnessing is a work of God.

Saturday 17th December
Matthew 1:1–17

An account of the genealogy of Jesus the Messiah, the son of David, the son of Abraham. Abraham was the father of Isaac, and Isaac the father of Jacob, and Jacob the father of Judah and his brothers, and Judah the father of Perez and Zerah by Tamar, and Perez the father of Hezron, and Hezron the father of Aram, and Aram the father of Aminadab, and Aminadab the father of Nahshon, and Nahshon the father of Salmon, and Salmon the father of Boaz by Rahab, and Boaz the father of Obed by Ruth, and Obed the father of Jesse, and Jesse the father of King David. And David was the father of Solomon by the wife of Uriah, and Solomon the father of Rehoboam, and Rehoboam the father of Abijah, and Abijah the father of Asaph, and Asaph the father of Jehoshaphat, and Jehoshaphat the father of Joram, and Joram the father of Uzziah, and Uzziah the father of Jotham, and Jotham the father of Ahaz, and Ahaz the father of Hezekiah, and Hezekiah the father of Manasseh, and Manasseh the father of Amos, and Amos the father of Josiah, and Josiah the father of Jechoniah and his brothers, at the time of the deportation to Babylon. And after the deportation to Babylon: Jechoniah was the father of Salathiel, and Salathiel the father of

Zerubbabel, and Zerubbabel the father of Abiud, and Abiud the father of Eliakim, and Eliakim the father of Azor, and Azor the father of Zadok, and Zadok the father of Achim, and Achim the father of Eliud, and Eliud the father of Eleazar, and Eleazar the father of Matthan, and Matthan the father of Jacob, and Jacob the father of Joseph the husband of Mary, of whom Jesus was born, who is called the Messiah. So all the generations from Abraham to David are fourteen generations; and from David to the deportation to Babylon, fourteen generations; and from the deportation to Babylon to the Messiah, fourteen generations.

- We all face the challenge to become our best selves. Family tradition and social expectations play their part here, but deepest down we need to know what God is inviting us to be. We are God's beloveds, and a high destiny awaits us. We are to reveal to the world something of God's own self.

- Today's reading looks unsparingly at Jesus' ancestry. Matthew points out that Jesus' forbears included children born of incest (Perez), of mixed races (Boaz), and of adultery (Solomon). God entered our human history with all the episodes that proud people would be ashamed of. Lord, teach me to accept my humanity, my genes, and my relatives, as you did.

The Fourth Week of Advent
December 18—December 24, 2016

Something to think and pray about each day this week:

What Are We Expecting?
How do we prepare our hearts for you, Jesus? Or do we understand our need to prepare? Are we more likely to hurry around once you're here, trying to focus on this guest we weren't expecting? Will we be ready when you appear there in the manger? Or will our hearts and minds be so focused on our immediate struggles that we're unprepared to receive eternal hope and grace? Will we recognize you? Or will we be looking for a savior of our own making? One who is powerful, maybe, who can rule the world by force if necessary? Will we be looking for a savior who looks like we do in race, culture, or religion? Will we stop and gaze upon you, forgetting everything else for just a few moments? Or will we be too distracted by credit card bills, the fallout of family gatherings, the extra pounds we've gained, and all the things we want to buy and do in the coming year? Will we journey through all sorts of weather and landscapes just to get a glimpse of you? Or if it's just too hard to get to the manger, will we flip through the TV channels one more time, get a snack, put on comfortable clothes,

and get lost in consoling fantasies? How will we prepare our hearts for the Christ Child?

—Vinita Hampton Wright, Loyola Press blogs

The Presence of God
"I stand at the door and knock," says the Lord. What
a wonderful privilege that the Lord of all creation desires to come to me. I welcome his presence.

Freedom
Saint Ignatius thought that a thick and shapeless tree
trunk would never believe that it could become a
statue, admired as a miracle of sculpture, and would
never submit itself to the chisel of the sculptor, who
sees by her genius what she can make of it.
I ask for the grace to let myself be shaped by my loving Creator.

Consciousness
Knowing that God loves me unconditionally, I can
afford to be honest about how I am. What are my
fears and desires? What do I expect from God? What
am I willing to give to God—from my emotions and
talents, thoughts and energy? And how do I feel now?
I share my feelings openly with the Lord.

The Word

I take my time to read the word of God, slowly, a few times, allowing myself to dwell on anything that strikes me. (Please turn to the Scripture on the following pages. Inspiration points are there should you need them. When you are ready, return here to continue.)

Conversation

Do I notice myself reacting as I pray with the word of God? Do I feel challenged, comforted, angry? Imagining Jesus sitting or standing by me, I speak out my feelings, as one trusted friend to another.

Conclusion

I thank God for these moments we have spent together and for any insights I may have been given concerning the text.

Sunday 18th December
Fourth Sunday of Advent
Matthew 1:18–24

Now the birth of Jesus the Messiah took place in this way. When his mother Mary had been engaged to Joseph, but before they lived together, she was found to be with child from the Holy Spirit. Her husband Joseph, being a righteous man and unwilling to expose her to public disgrace, planned to dismiss her quietly. But just when he had resolved to do this, an angel of the Lord appeared to him in a dream and said, "Joseph, son of David, do not be afraid to take Mary as your wife, for the child conceived in her is from the Holy Spirit. She will bear a son, and you are to name him Jesus, for he will save his people from their sins." All this took place to fulfill what had been spoken by the Lord through the prophet: "Look, the virgin shall conceive and bear a son, and they shall name him Emmanuel, which means, 'God is with us.'" When Joseph awoke from sleep, he did as the angel of the Lord commanded him; he took her as his wife.

- Joseph is faced with a heartbreaking dilemma. His life is in turmoil because he loves Mary so much. Let me imagine for a few moments how welcome the angel's message must have been to him! How quickly he acts, allowing himself to follow his heart and not allowing his sense of legal obligation to rule.

• How often in Scripture does the quiet prompting of the Spirit come from within, in the form of a dream. How sensitive must the dreamers have been, to recognize the Spirit in their hearts. Do I invite the Spirit to prompt me? How ready am I to hear what the Spirit might suggest?

Monday 19th December
Luke 1:5–25

In the days of King Herod of Judea, there was a priest named Zechariah, who belonged to the priestly order of Abijah. His wife was a descendant of Aaron, and her name was Elizabeth. Both of them were righteous before God, living blamelessly according to all the commandments and regulations of the Lord. But they had no children, because Elizabeth was barren, and both were getting on in years. Once when he was serving as priest before God and his section was on duty, he was chosen by lot, according to the custom of the priesthood, to enter the sanctuary of the Lord and offer incense. Now at the time of the incense offering, the whole assembly of the people was praying outside. Then there appeared to him an angel of the Lord, standing at the right side of the altar of incense. When Zechariah saw him, he was terrified; and fear overwhelmed him. But the angel said to him, "Do not be afraid, Zechariah, for your prayer has been heard. Your wife Elizabeth will bear you a son, and you will name him John. You will have joy and gladness, and many will rejoice at his birth, for he will be great in the sight of the Lord. He must never drink wine or strong drink; even before his birth he will be filled with the Holy Spirit. He will turn many of the people of Israel to the Lord their God. With the spirit and power of Elijah he will go before him, to turn the hearts of parents to their children, and the disobedient to the wisdom of the righteous, to make ready a people prepared for the Lord." Zechariah said to the angel, "How will I know that this is so? For I am an old man, and my wife is getting on in years." The angel replied, "I am Gabriel. I stand in the presence of God, and I have been sent to speak to you and to bring you this good news. But now, because you did not believe my words, which will be fulfilled in their time, you will become mute, unable to speak, until the day these things occur." Meanwhile the people were waiting for Zechariah, and wondered at his delay in the sanctuary. When he did come out, he could not speak to them, and they realized that he had seen a vision in the sanctuary. He kept motioning to them and remained unable to speak. When his time of service was ended, he went to his home. After those days his wife Elizabeth conceived, and for five months she remained in seclusion. She said, "This is what the Lord has done for me when he looked favorably on me and took away the disgrace I have endured among my people."

- Despite all his prayer, along with reassurance from the angel, Zechariah is unable to put his trust and faith in God's way. The consequence is months of isolation, during which Zechariah is unable to communicate. Despite the man's obstinacy, God's favor is seen in the birth of Zechariah's son. Elizabeth has no difficulty acknowledging the source of new life, saying, "This is what the Lord has done for me." This Advent day, can I reflect back on my life and say likewise?

- Between today and Christmas Day, the liturgy features three biblical women who become pregnant against all the odds: Elizabeth, mother of John the Baptist; the unnamed mother of Samson; and Hannah, mother of Samuel. They remind us that God is in control of the human story and intervenes graciously in favor of the helpless and despised.

Tuesday 20th December
Luke 1:26–38

In the sixth month the angel Gabriel was sent by God to a town in Galilee called Nazareth, to a virgin engaged to a man whose name was Joseph, of the house of David. The virgin's name was Mary. And he came to her and said, "Greetings, favored one! The Lord is with you." But she was much perplexed by his words and pondered what sort of greeting this might be. The angel said to her, "Do not be afraid, Mary, for you have found favor with God. And now, you will conceive in your womb and bear a son, and you will name him Jesus. He will be great, and will be called the Son of the Most High, and the Lord God will give to him the throne of his ancestor David. He will reign over the house of Jacob forever, and of his kingdom there will be no end." Mary said to the angel, "How can this be, since I am a virgin?" The angel said to her, "The Holy Spirit will come upon you, and the power of the Most High will overshadow you; therefore the child to be born will be holy; he will be called Son of God. And now, your relative Elizabeth in her old age has also conceived a son; and this is the sixth month for her who was said to be barren. For nothing will be impossible with God." Then Mary said, "Here am I, the servant of the Lord; let it be with me according to your word." Then the angel departed from her.

• Mary, the young girl of no status, from the village of Nazareth, an utterly insignificant place, is signaled out, called, chosen, and overshadowed with

God's Spirit. Her response moves from fear to total trust in God's inscrutable designs.

- Lord, may I grow each day in trusting your amazing annunciation to me: I am your "highly favored" one, and I am not to be afraid. You rejoice in me! In the busyness of life, keep these thoughts before me. Like Mary, may I be ready to play my part in bringing you to birth.

Wednesday 21st December
Luke 1:39–45

In those days Mary set out and went with haste to a Judean town in the hill country, where she entered the house of Zechariah and greeted Elizabeth. When Elizabeth heard Mary's greeting, the child leaped in her womb. And Elizabeth was filled with the Holy Spirit and exclaimed with a loud cry, "Blessed are you among women, and blessed is the fruit of your womb. And why has this happened to me, that the mother of my Lord comes to me? For as soon as I heard the sound of your greeting, the child in my womb leaped for joy. And blessed is she who believed that there would be a fulfillment of what was spoken to her by the Lord."

- I marvel at the instinct and insight of mothers. While husband Zechariah is baffled and struck dumb and foster father Joseph has misgivings, it is a woman, Elizabeth, herself pregnant, who recognizes the action of the Lord in her young cousin. She is given the special grace of an intimate appreciation of what is happening and who is really present. In life do I always appreciate what is happening and who is really present?

- John leaped for joy in the presence of his Lord. Centuries earlier, King David "danced before the Lord with all his might." The psalmist tells us to "shout for joy." Saint Paul urges us to "sing and make melody to the Lord with all our heart." It is the child in us who can truly be open to God's constant invitation to be born again and to be part of the creation which is itself constantly being recreated. The child in us is free to rejoice.

Thursday 22nd December
Luke 1:46–56

And Mary said, "My soul magnifies the Lord, and my spirit rejoices in God my Savior, for he has looked with favor on the lowliness of his servant. Surely, from now on all generations will call me blessed; for the Mighty One has done great things for me, and holy is his name. His mercy is for those who fear him from generation to generation. He has shown strength with his arm; he has scattered the proud in the thoughts of their hearts. He has brought down the powerful from their thrones, and lifted up the lowly; he has filled the hungry with good things, and sent the rich away empty. He has helped his servant Israel, in remembrance of his mercy, according to the promise he made to our ancestors, to Abraham and to his descendants forever." And Mary remained with Elizabeth about three months and then returned to her home.

- I imagine that I am invited to stay with Elizabeth and Mary for the three months they spent together. I observe what they say and do, and how quietly happy they both are, as they each carry the mystery of God in their wombs.

- With Mary, I count my blessings, not as a matter of pride or achievement but to recognize where God is at work in my life. Pride and humility are in the picture as Mary prays her Magnificat. Mary rejoices in being a blessed, lowly servant. I think of how this description relates to how I am now.

Friday 23rd December
Luke 1:57–66

Now the time came for Elizabeth to give birth, and she bore a son. Her neighbors and relatives heard that the Lord had shown his great mercy to her, and they rejoiced with her. On the eighth day they came to circumcise the child, and they were going to name him Zechariah after his father. But his mother said, "No; he is to be called John." They said to her, "None of your relatives has this name." Then they began motioning to his father to find out what name he wanted to give him. He asked for a writing tablet and wrote, "His name is John." And all of them were amazed. Immediately his mouth was opened and his tongue freed, and he began to speak, praising God. Fear came over all their neighbors, and all these things were talked about throughout the entire hill country of Judea. All who heard them pondered them and said, "What then will this child become?" For, indeed, the hand of the Lord was with him.

- How did Elizabeth know that the child was to be called John? Did a small voice tell her this? Do I listen for the small voice that tells me what to do? Elizabeth and Mary were ordinary people, just as I am. God speaks to me as God spoke to them.

- Even in his old age, Zechariah was ready to break from the old patterns. I ask for the help that I need to step away from the usual patterns and to follow God's call. I pray for all children: may the joy and hope that they experience live and grow into a deep appreciation of God's goodness.

Saturday 24th December

Luke 1:67–79

Then his father Zechariah was filled with the Holy Spirit and spoke this prophecy: "Blessed be the Lord God of Israel, for he has looked favorably on his people and redeemed them. He has raised up a mighty savior for us in the house of his servant David, as he spoke through the mouth of his holy prophets from of old, that we would be saved from our enemies and from the hand of all who hate us. Thus he has shown the mercy promised to our ancestors, and has remembered his holy covenant, the oath that he swore to our ancestor Abraham, to grant us that we, being rescued from the hands of our enemies, might serve him without fear, in holiness and righteousness before him all our days. And you, child, will be called the prophet of the Most High; for you will go before the Lord to prepare his ways, to give knowledge of salvation to his people by the forgiveness of their sins. By the tender mercy of our God, the dawn from on high will break upon us, to give light to those who sit in darkness and in the shadow of death, to guide our feet into the way of peace."

- Zechariah is profoundly aware of his heritage and sees God's action in the past as having promise for the future. I draw encouragement from my own story, allowing God to bless me with hope and confidence in continued blessing.

- Allow this psalm of thanks and praise to express what you feel and believe. Zechariah made this prayer for his son. It was a prayer grown and made in love. We are now the ones who go before the Lord; our love and care can become the dawn breaking into others' lives, giving light to all in darkness. We are the ones to walk with the peace that calms those around us and guides them on their journey. Take what is suitable from this great prayer, said each morning throughout the church, and allow it to link you with the living Christ.

December 25—December 31, 2016

Something to think and pray about each day this week:

Details and Mystery

Some years, during Advent, the concreteness of the nativity story—how normal, how tangible it is—draws me in. The awkward unease of late pregnancy. The human need for shelter and rest. Straw, wood, pieces of cloth. The scent of barn animals. A newborn baby's cry. But this year, it's the swirl of mystery that hovers above and through the narrative that most captures my imagination. In an Advent homily, my priest quoted a theologian who said that thinking about God is like trying to draw a picture of a bird in flight. "You end up with details of its wings caught in a certain position, feathers, eyes, claws frozen in place for careful scrutiny," he explained. "Or you end up with a blur that loses all detail, but captures speed and movement." We're all theologians, he said, and we all envision various concepts of God in detail and others in motion. Do we choose one picture over another, or somehow hold both in tension?

—Jennifer Grant, *Wholehearted Living*

The Presence of God

To be present is to arrive as one is and open up to the other.

At this instant, as I arrive here, God is present waiting for me.

God always arrives before me, desiring to connect with me

even more than my most intimate friend.

I take a moment and greet my loving God.

Freedom

I am free. When I look at these words in writing, they seem to create in me a feeling of awe. Yes, a wonderful feeling of freedom. Thank you, God.

Consciousness

To be conscious about something is to be aware of it. Dear Lord, help me to remember that You gave me life.

Thank you for the gift of life.

Teach me to slow down, to be still and enjoy the pleasures created for me. To be aware of the beauty that surrounds me. The marvel of mountains, the calmness of lakes, the fragility of a flower petal. I need to remember that all these things come from you.

The Word
The Word of God comes down to us through the Scriptures. May the Holy Spirit enlighten my mind and my heart to respond to the Gospel teachings. (Please turn to the Scripture on the following pages. Inspiration points are there should you need them. When you are ready, return here to continue.)

Conversation
I begin to talk to Jesus about the piece of Scripture I have just read. What part of it strikes a chord in me? Perhaps the words of a friend—or some story I have heard recently—will slowly rise to the surface in my consciousness. If so, does the story throw light on what the Scripture passage may be trying to say to me?

Conclusion
Glory be to the Father, and to the Son, and to the Holy Spirit,
As it was in the beginning, is now and ever shall be,
World without end. Amen.

Sunday 25th December
The Nativity of the Lord

John 1:1–18

In the beginning was the Word, and the Word was with God, and the Word was God. He was in the beginning with God. All things came into being through him, and without him not one thing came into being. What has come into being in him was life, and the life was the light of all people. The light shines in the darkness, and the darkness did not overcome it. There was a man sent from God, whose name was John. He came as a witness to testify to the light, so that all might believe through him. He himself was not the light, but he came to testify to the light. The true light, which enlightens everyone, was coming into the world. He was in the world, and the world came into being through him; yet the world did not know him. He came to what was his own, and his own people did not accept him. But to all who received him, who believed in his name, he gave power to become children of God, who were born, not of blood or of the will of the flesh or of the will of man, but of God. And the Word became flesh and lived among us, and we have seen his glory, the glory as of a father's only son, full of grace and truth. (John testified to him and cried out, "This was he of whom

I said, 'He who comes after me ranks ahead of me because he was before me.'") From his fullness we have all received, grace upon grace. The law indeed was given through Moses; grace and truth came through Jesus Christ. No one has ever seen God. It is God the only Son, who is close to the Father's heart, who has made him known.

- In this hymn, which introduces the fourth Gospel, John proclaims the faith that marks us as Christian. We believe that Jesus is the Word of God, God's perfect expression. "No one has ever seen God. It is God the only Son, who is close to the Father's heart, who has made him known." Lord, in the year that starts tonight, let me grow in the knowledge of God. May I receive of your fullness, grace upon grace. You took on this mortal flesh for me and lived among us. May this coming year bring me closer to you.

- In this time of prayer, I let what is at the heart of God reveal itself to me: life and light for all. I acknowledge what comes between me and this life God offers. I identify what darkens my heart and narrows my vision. The goodness and generosity of God are here for me as God longs to become present in the world through me.

Monday 26th December
Matthew 10:17–22

Jesus said, "Beware of them, for they will hand you over to councils and flog you in their synagogues; and you will be dragged before governors and kings because of me, as a testimony to them and the Gentiles. When they hand you over, do not worry about how you are to speak or what you are to say; for what you are to say will be given to you at that time; for it is not you who speak, but the Spirit of your Father speaking through you. Brother will betray brother to death, and a father his child, and children will rise against parents and have them put to death; and you will be hated by all because of my name. But the one who endures to the end will be saved."

- The following advice, attributed to Saint Teresa of Ávila, says that endurance gains us everything:

  Let nothing disturb you.
  Let nothing frighten you.
  All things are passing.
  God never changes.
  Patient endurance attains all things.
  God alone suffices.

- Lord, today we pray for those who are tormented in your name. Martyrs continue to lay down their lives for you, even today. There are also the subtler trials that believers endure: scientific scorn, media distortion, opposition to faith perspectives. Give us the gift of endurance in all of this.

Tuesday 27th December

John 20:1a, 2–8

Mary Magdalene ran and went to Simon Peter and the other disciple, the one whom Jesus loved, and said to them, "They have taken the Lord out of the tomb, and we do not know where they have laid him." Then Peter and the other disciple set out and went towards the tomb. The two were running together, but the other disciple outran Peter and reached the tomb first. He bent down to look in and saw the linen wrappings lying there, but he did not go in. Then Simon Peter came, following him, and went into the tomb. He saw the linen wrappings lying there, and the cloth that had been on Jesus' head, not lying with the linen wrappings but rolled up in a place by itself. Then the other disciple, who reached the tomb first, also went in, and he saw and believed.

- Risen Lord, help me see beyond the obvious and understand your ways. You show me you are alive and active in my moments of joyous discovery, in touches of gladness, in enriching encounters, and in the kindnesses of others. Always you come delicately. As poet Gerard Manley Hopkins wrote: "I greet you the days I meet you, and bless when I understand."

- John describes how the disciple saw and believed. However, John later points out that it is not enough for us to believe; we must spread the good news, as he himself did: "We are writing these things so that our joy may be complete." I notice that sharing good news brings joy to the sharer as well as to the receiver. Do I experience this?

Wednesday 28th December
Matthew 2:13–18

Now after they had left, an angel of the Lord appeared to Joseph in a dream and said, "Get up, take the child and his mother, and flee to Egypt, and remain there until I tell you; for Herod is about to search for the child, to destroy him." Then Joseph got up, took the child and his mother by night, and went to Egypt, and remained there until the death of Herod. This was to fulfill what had been spoken by the Lord through the prophet, "Out of Egypt I have called my son." When Herod saw that he had been tricked by the wise men, he was infuriated, and he sent and killed all the children in and around Bethlehem who were two years old or under, according to the time that he had learned from the wise men. Then was fulfilled what had been spoken through the prophet Jeremiah: "A voice was heard in Ramah, wailing and loud lamentation, Rachel weeping for her children; she refused to be consoled, because they are no more."

- This is a painful story. What difficult news the angel brings: Joseph and his tiny family have to become refugees and go by night to a foreign land. We ask for his strength of soul today to do what we can to help the world's refugees.

- This morning I pray for the mourning mothers of the Holy Land, weeping to this day for their dead children, because they are no more. Arabs and Jews, all of them one people—Semites—continue to kill one another, in the delusion that bombs and blood will help. I pray for a spirit of peace there.

Thursday 29th December
Luke 2:22–35

When the time came for their purification according to the law of Moses, they brought him up to Jerusalem to present him to the Lord (as it is written in the law of the Lord, "Every firstborn male shall be designated as holy to the Lord"), and they offered a sacrifice according to what is stated in the law of the Lord, "a pair of turtledoves or two young pigeons." Now there was a man in Jerusalem whose name was Simeon; this man was righteous and devout, looking forward to the consolation of Israel, and the Holy Spirit rested on him. It had been revealed to him by the Holy Spirit that he would not see death before he had seen the Lord's Messiah. Guided by the Spirit,

Simeon came into the temple; and when the parents brought in the child Jesus, to do for him what was customary under the law, Simeon took him in his arms and praised God, saying, "Master, now you are dismissing your servant in peace, according to your word; for my eyes have seen your salvation, which you have prepared in the presence of all peoples, a light for revelation to the Gentiles and for glory to your people Israel." And the child's father and mother were amazed at what was being said about him. Then Simeon blessed them and said to his mother Mary, "This child is destined for the falling and the rising of many in Israel, and to be a sign that will be opposed so that the inner thoughts of many will be revealed—and a sword will pierce your own soul too."

- Simeon sings his song of farewell after a lifetime of watching for the sign of God's salvation. Attuned to the Holy Spirit, he identifies Jesus from the many children who have come up to Jerusalem. Jesus comes not in power but as a babe in his mother's arms. He comes as a light for all who are in darkness. Lord, may your Holy Spirit rest on me today. Like Simeon, may I recognize that you have come in the form of a vulnerable child.

- Lord, in Simeon I see hope richly rewarded. The years of waiting did not blunt the edge of his faith. His hope and yearning kept him alive to the promptings of God, ready to hear God's voice when it came. Grant that I may learn from him.

Friday 30th December
The Holy Family of Jesus, Mary, and Joseph
Matthew 2:13–15, 19–23

Now after they had left, an angel of the Lord appeared to Joseph in a dream and said, "Get up, take the child and his mother, and flee to Egypt, and remain there until I tell you; for Herod is about to search for the child, to destroy him." Then Joseph got up, took the child and his mother by night, and went to Egypt, and remained there until the death of Herod. This was to fulfill what had been spoken by the Lord through the prophet, "Out of Egypt I have called my son." When Herod died, an angel of the Lord suddenly appeared in a dream to Joseph in Egypt and said, "Get up, take the child and his mother, and go to the land of Israel, for those who were seeking the child's life are dead." Then Joseph got up, took the child and his mother, and went to the land of Israel. But when he heard that Archelaus was ruling over Judea in place of his father Herod, he was afraid to go there. And after being warned in a dream, he went away to the district of Galilee. There he made his home in a town called Nazareth, so that what had been spoken through the prophets might be fulfilled, "He will be called a Nazorean."

- We see that on a number of occasions, angels direct Joseph in his dreams. But we also find that he uses his own common sense! He is cautious that the son of Herod will be as bad as the father and so takes precautions. Joseph is a model of protection and devotion as a husband and a father. Lord, may I be as caring of others as he is.

- Like any newly married couple, Mary and Joseph have their dreams and hopes. He is a skilled carpenter, so their future seems secure. Then, suddenly, everything falls apart: the birth in a stable, the flight into Egypt, and the long wait until they can return to Galilee. But in all the mess, they stay faithful to one another and they bring up the Son of God. Lord, may we support family life no matter how much it is threatened.

Saturday 31st December
John 1:1–18

In the beginning was the Word, and the Word was with God, and the Word was God. He was in the beginning with God. All things came into being through him, and without him not one thing came into being. What has come into being in him was life, and the life was the light of all people. The light shines in the darkness, and the darkness did not overcome it. There was a man sent from God, whose name was John. He came as a witness to testify to the light, so that all might believe through him. He himself was not the light, but he came to testify to the light. The true light, which enlightens everyone, was coming into the world. He was in the world, and the world came into being through him; yet the world did not know him. He came to what was his own, and his own people did not accept him. But to all who received him, who believed in his name, he gave power to become children of God, who were born, not of blood or of the will of the flesh or of the will of man, but of God. And the Word became flesh and lived among us, and we have seen his glory, the glory as of a father's only son, full of grace and truth. (John testified to him and cried out, "This was he of whom I said, 'He who comes after me ranks ahead of me because he was before me.'") From his fullness we have all received, grace upon grace. The law indeed was given through Moses; grace and truth came through Jesus Christ. No one has ever seen God. It is God the only Son, who is close to the Father's heart, who has made him known.

- "The light shines in the darkness, and the darkness did not overcome it." Facing a new calendar year, may we shine with divine light. May this light shine within, so that we believe we are the children of God, loved to the core. May we in turn love others limitlessly and so bring them light and consolation in their everyday lives.

- One theologian wrote, "I searched for God in the heavens but found he had fallen to earth, so I must seek him among my friends." Lord, Emmanuel, I draw near to you today as I celebrate your birth. I thank you for moving house, so to speak, and locating yourself so fully in our human story of loneliness, pain, frailty, and fragility.

The Second Week of Christmas/Epiphany
January 1—January 8, 2017

Something to think and pray about each day this week:

Where Holy Encounter Leads
The story of Christ's coming as a child is filled with miracles: angels coming in person and in dreams; a child born to a virgin; a mysterious star; holy secrets spoken to shepherds and wise men. The glory of this coming has the power to entrance us year after year as we make the journey through Advent and find ourselves, yet again, at the manger. But the child grew up, was baptized by John, and embarked on a life that few if any could fathom or desire. And for each person who encountered this life of God-among-us, the glory and gratitude led also to personal pilgrimage and transformation. Even now, these glorious and enlightening events create holy encounter, which leads us to engagement with God that is personal. Mary and Joseph were forever changed, as were other players in this sacred drama, from the shepherds to John the Baptist and those who would become Jesus' disciples. They invite us by their examples to be courageous enough to stand at the manger but then follow the child to wherever he desires to take us.

—The Editors

The Presence of God

Be still and know that I am God. Lord, may your Spirit guide me to seek your loving presence more and more. For it is there I find rest and refreshment from this busy world.

Freedom

By God's grace I was born to live in freedom. Free to enjoy the pleasures He created for me. Dear Lord, grant that I may live as You intended, with complete confidence in Your Loving care.

Consciousness

In God's loving presence I unwind the past day, starting from now and looking back, moment by moment.
I gather in all the goodness and light, in gratitude.
I attend to the shadows and what they say to me, seeking healing, courage, forgiveness.

The Word

The Word of God comes to us through the Scriptures. May the Holy Spirit enlighten my mind and heart to respond to the Gospel teachings. (Please turn to the Scripture on the following pages. Inspiration points are there should you need them. When you are ready, return here to continue.)

Conversation

Jesus, you always welcomed little children when you walked on this earth. Teach me to have a childlike trust in you. To live in the knowledge that you will never abandon me.

Conclusion

Glory be to the Father, and to the Son, and to the Holy Spirit,
As it was in the beginning, is now and ever shall be,
World without end. Amen.

Sunday 1st January
Solemnity of Mary, the
Holy Mother of God

Luke 2:16–21

So they went with haste and found Mary and Joseph, and the child lying in the manger. When they saw this, they made known what had been told them about this child; and all who heard it were amazed at what the shepherds told them. But Mary treasured all these words and pondered them in her heart. The shepherds returned, glorifying and praising God for all they had heard and seen, as it had been told them. After eight days had passed, it was time to circumcise the child; and he was called Jesus, the name given by the angel before he was conceived in the womb.

- According to the story, an angel had months ago appeared to Mary, and more angels had now appeared to the shepherds. All the heavenly messengers had conveyed an assurance: "You are going to see that God has sent into the world a prince from heaven's kingdom." The promise filled all with anticipation and the fulfillment filled all—Mary and the shepherds—with thanksgiving. Placing myself alongside Mary before the child, I try to open my heart to thanksgiving for all that God has done in my life.

• We start the year, as we start life, under the protection of a mother. Today we celebrate the most passionate and enduring of all human relationships, that of mother and child. As Mary looked at her baby and gave him her breast, she knew that there was a dimension here beyond her guessing. Christians thought about it for three centuries before the Council of Ephesus, in which they dared to consecrate the title **θεοτοκος**, mother of god. Like Mary, I treasure the words spoken about Jesus and ponder them in my heart.

Monday 2nd January
John 1:19–28

This is the testimony given by John when the Jews sent priests and Levites from Jerusalem to ask him, "Who are you?" He confessed and did not deny it, but confessed, "I am not the Messiah." And they asked him, "What then? Are you Elijah?" He said, "I am not." "Are you the prophet?" He answered, "No." Then they said to him, "Who are you? Let us have an answer for those who sent us. What do you say about yourself?" He said, "I am the voice of one crying out in the wilderness, 'Make straight the way of the Lord,' as the prophet Isaiah said." Now they had been sent from the Pharisees. They asked him, "Why then are you baptizing if you are neither the Messiah, nor Elijah, nor the prophet?" John answered them, "I baptize with water. Among you stands one whom you do not know, the one who is coming after me; I am not worthy to untie the thong of his sandal." This took place in Bethany across the Jordan where John was baptizing.

- Although he prepared the way for Jesus, John acknowledges that he did not know whom to expect. As I do my best, in my way, to prepare the way for Jesus, I cannot always know just what to be ready for.

- John remained active and vigilant. I pray that I may find the balance to stay occupied in God's service without letting my occupations overwhelm me.

Tuesday 3rd January
John 1:29–34

The next day John saw Jesus coming toward him and declared, "Here is the Lamb of God who takes away the sin of the world! This is he of whom I said, 'After me comes a man who ranks ahead of me because he was before me.' I myself did not know him; but I came baptizing with water for this reason, that he might be revealed to Israel." And John testified, "I saw the Spirit descending from heaven like a dove, and it remained on him. I myself did not know him, but the one who sent me to baptize with water said to me, 'He on whom you see the Spirit descend and remain is the one who baptizes with the Holy Spirit.' And I myself have seen and have testified that this is the Son of God."

- John's mission has reached its completion. His function was to point people in the direction of Jesus, the Lamb of God. With these words John draws back the curtain, and Jesus takes center stage in our human story, inviting us to be with him.

- The witness of John the Baptist depended on what was revealed to him in his prayer and on what he saw with his eyes. Bless me now, Lord, to recognize more clearly where you are moving in my life.

Wednesday 4th January
John 1:35–42

The next day John again was standing with two of his disciples, and as he watched Jesus walk by, he exclaimed, "Look, here is the Lamb of God!" The two disciples heard him say this, and they followed Jesus. When Jesus turned and saw them following, he said to them, "What are you looking for?" They said to him, "Rabbi" (which translated means Teacher), "where are you staying?" He said to them, "Come and see." They came and saw where he was staying, and they remained with him that day. It was about four o'clock in the afternoon. One of the two who heard John speak and followed him was Andrew, Simon Peter's brother. He first found his brother Simon and said to him, "We have found the Messiah" (which translated means Anointed). He brought Simon to Jesus, who looked at him and said, "You are Simon son of John. You are to be called Cephas" (which translated means Peter).

- John the Baptist, who has an immense following in Jerusalem, does something remarkable here. He points his followers toward Jesus, the Lamb of God. With John's blessing, they walk away from him and follow Jesus. John is not the light but has come to bear witness to the light. He is happy to see his followers leave and to experience his own influence diminishing, because he is witnessing to Jesus. If we bring our ego to people, we bring death. If we bring Jesus, we bring life.

- I hear Jesus ask me, "What are you looking for?" I take time to answer with what is deep in my heart. If I cannot find words, I stay with my mood, being present to Jesus, who knows and loves me. I listen for his invitation to draw closer: "Come and see."

Thursday 5th January
John 1:43–51

The next day Jesus decided to go to Galilee. He found Philip and said to him, "Follow me." Now

Philip was from Bethsaida, the city of Andrew and Peter. Philip found Nathanael and said to him, "We have found him about whom Moses in the law and also the prophets wrote, Jesus son of Joseph from Nazareth." Nathanael said to him, "Can anything good come out of Nazareth?" Philip said to him, "Come and see." When Jesus saw Nathanael coming toward him, he said of him, "Here is truly an Israelite in whom there is no deceit!" Nathanael asked him, "Where did you get to know me?" Jesus answered, "I saw you under the fig tree before Philip called you." Nathanael replied, "Rabbi, you are the Son of God! You are the King of Israel!" Jesus answered, "Do you believe because I told you that I saw you under the fig tree? You will see greater things than these." And he said to him, "Very truly, I tell you, you will see heaven opened and the angels of God ascending and descending upon the Son of Man."

- "Can anything good come out of Nazareth?" How often, Lord, have I tried to pigeonhole people by looking down on their gender, origin, race, or family. Nathanael (identified with Bartholomew from the ninth century on) could have missed the chance to meet you, if not for Philip's gentle invitation: Come and see. Save me, Lord, from the stupidity of those who try to seem smart by despising others. May I heed Philip and fill my vision with you.

- "Where did you get to know me?" Nathanial is surprised not because Jesus saw him under the fig tree but because Jesus read the thoughts of his innermost heart. As I sit with you, Jesus, I ponder, How do you see me? How do you read my innermost heart?

Friday 6th January
Mark 1:7–11

John proclaimed, "The one who is more powerful than I is coming after me; I am not worthy to stoop down and untie the thong of his sandals. I have baptized you with water; but he will baptize you with the Holy Spirit." In those days Jesus came from Nazareth of Galilee and was baptized by John in the Jordan. And just as he was coming up out of the water, he saw the heavens torn apart and the Spirit descending like a dove on him. And a voice came from heaven, "You are my Son, the Beloved; with you I am well pleased."

- Imagine yourself witnessing the scene, perhaps standing in the shallows, the water flowing around your ankles. Picture the scene and allow it to unfold. What is it like? The young man from Nazareth joins the queue waiting for John's baptism, a symbol of purifying but also of birth: coming up out of the waters of the womb into a new life as God's beloved child.

- Jesus' baptism gives us a window into a powerful religious moment. Jesus knows his identity. The imprint of the Spirit has sealed his life. Lord, remind me that I bear your seal of approval. I am marked by your Spirit, called to participate in your mission as your beloved son or daughter.

Saturday 7th January
John 2:1–11

On the third day there was a wedding in Cana of Galilee, and the mother of Jesus was there. Jesus and his disciples had also been invited to the wedding. When the wine gave out, the mother of Jesus said to him, "They have no wine." And Jesus said to her, "Woman, what concern is that to you and to me? My hour has not yet come." His mother said to the servants, "Do whatever he tells you." Now standing there were six stone water jars for the Jewish rites of purification, each holding twenty or thirty gallons. Jesus said to them, "Fill the jars with water." And they filled them up to the brim. He said to them, "Now draw some out, and take it to the chief steward." So they took it. When the steward tasted the water that had become wine, and did not know where it came from (though the servants who had drawn the water knew), the steward called the bridegroom and said to him, "Everyone serves the good wine first, and then the inferior wine after the guests have become drunk. But you have kept the good wine until now." Jesus did this, the first of his signs, in Cana of Galilee, and revealed his glory; and his disciples believed in him.

- It appears that Jesus needed a push from someone who loved and knew him and knew his purpose in the world. Lord, help me listen when others nudge me toward my work and my calling.

- God sent Jesus into this human life, yet Jesus had to embrace his life mission day by day. When was the last time I purposefully embraced a task or goal because I recognized that it was God's will for me and part of my life calling?

Sunday 8th January
The Epiphany of the Lord
Matthew 2:1–12

In the time of King Herod, after Jesus was born in Bethlehem of Judea, wise men from the East came to Jerusalem, asking, "Where is the child who has been born king of the Jews? For we observed his star at its rising, and have come to pay him homage." When King Herod heard this, he was frightened, and all Jerusalem with him; and calling together all the chief priests and scribes of the people, he inquired of them where the Messiah was to be born. They told him, "In Bethlehem of Judea; for so it has been written by the prophet: 'And you, Bethlehem, in the land of Judah, are by no means least among the rulers of Judah; for from you shall come a ruler who is to shepherd my people Israel.'" Then Herod secretly called for the wise men and learned from them the exact time when the star had appeared. Then he sent them to Bethlehem, saying, "Go and search diligently for the child; and when you have found him, bring me word so that I may also go and pay him homage." When they had heard the king, they set out; and there, ahead of them, went the star that they had seen at its rising, until it stopped over the place where the child was. When they saw that the star had stopped, they were overwhelmed with joy. On entering the house, they saw the child with Mary his mother; and they knelt down and paid him homage. Then, opening their treasure chests, they offered him gifts of gold, frankincense, and myrrh. And having been warned in a dream not to return to Herod, they left for their own country by another road.

- The wise men are remembered for their gifts. They highlight that each of us has gifts we can bring to God. The gift most worth giving at any age is our love. In prayer ask God to accept your love for husband or wife, friend, child, neighborhood. Think of those you love, and bring your love for them to the crib where Jesus lies. The Magi are remembered also for their journey and their search for God. A star guided them. In prayer, can we be grateful for those whose stars brought us to God—through their love, teaching, and example?

- This is the full unveiling (epiphany) of a mystery: the Lord has come among us to take an intimate hand in the future of the human race. We have God's word in Scripture: "I am about to do a new thing." I try to allow this to sink in.

Now, as
your brea
for *breat*
the same
God's Sp
come floc

- Now mov
  the Spirit
  of stillnes
  word from

Scripture

Matthew 2:7–

Then Herod
learned from
appeared. Th
"Go and searc
have found h
go and pay hi
king, they set
star that they
over the place

Reflect

- It may be h
  who have cr
  ly those wh

Welcome
with the l
year, we a
Magi (or v
you pray
that you v
paring thr
We also h
a deeper a
Consider

- Decide
  the ret
  minut

- Plan w

- Know
  and gr
  for the
  desire

- Before
  you to
  all th
  retrea

breathe in, let your attention follow
into your chest. In Hebrew, the words
nd *spirit*, as in the *Holy Spirit*, are
imagine breathing in God's breath,
, and letting the center of yourself be-
d with the Spirit's warmth and light.

our focus from your own breathing to
ting at the heart of you, in that place
From that still point, listen to God's
Matthew's Gospel.

cretly called for the wise men and
em the exact time when the star had
he sent them to Bethlehem, saying,
diligently for the child; and when you
, bring me word so that I may also
homage." When they had heard the
t; and there, ahead of them, went the
ad seen at its rising, until it stopped
here the child was.

pful to reflect on the many people
ssed our path in life and especial-
have walked with us in our faith

An Advent Retreat

Welcome to this year's Advent retreat, "Journeying with the Magi." To help and guide our prayer this year, we are reflecting on the Christmas story of the Magi (or wise men) from Saint Matthew's Gospel. As you pray with the material presented here, we hope that you will grow more aware of God at work, preparing through the centuries for the birth of his Son. We also hope that, at the same time, you'll come to a deeper awareness of God at work in your own life. Consider these points as you begin:

- Decide how long you will devote to each session of the retreat. Each session is designed to last 20–25 minutes.

- Plan which time of day you will pray the retreat.

- Know why you are making the retreat. What gifts and graces do you hope to receive? Begin by asking for the graces—the help and gifts from God—you desire.

- Before starting, become aware of God welcoming you to meet him in this way, and be conscious of all those around the world who are praying this retreat alongside you.

Introduction

An Advent retreat is a time of spiritual attentiveness so as to be more ready for the arrival of Christ in our lives this year. If you don't like the word *retreat*, then we can call this whole journey, with a little play on words, an Advent adventure of readiness.

To enter this adventure, we will reflect on some moments in the famous Christmas story of the Magi, or wise men, from Saint Matthew's Gospel. It is of course very well known, and much loved by children, because it lends itself so easily to dramatization. But in fact it's a drama of adult faith, as we shall see. Various moments in this narrative will offer us starting points for reflection and for personal prayer.

How are we to approach this adventure of meditation and prayer? Perhaps the first and most fundamental invitation of a retreat is simply to slow down. "The world is too much with us," said the poet Wordsworth, and there has never been so much world! So we need to escape the fragmentation and find something of simplicity. We need to retreat from the daily bustle and create some silence and stillness.

Notice those four qualities beginning with S: *slowness, simplicity, silence, stillness.* And we could add *self-patience* because it takes time to slow down. Most people need some skills of stillness in order to reach, gradually, a certain receptivity toward God.

What do we mean by skills of stillness? Some of them may be familiar to you. Simply listening to all the sounds around and letting that center you. Or paying attention to the coming and going of your breath. Or repeating some word or expression such as "Come, Lord Jesus." Or watching the flame of a candle, letting it focus your attention and banish other thoughts or sensations. See what helps you. Remember: it is not a question of technique but of readiness. Readiness for God.

We start with some practical suggestions that might help you if you haven't made a retreat like this before or might act as reminders if you have. As you begin each session of the retreat, use the Stillness Exercise provided to prepare yourself for this time of encounter with God. In order to deepen your inner silence, close your eyes and express within yourself a prayer of desire to discover what God wants you to discover in this meditation. Allow that prayer of petition to lead you into reverence and hope. Stay there for as long as you can.

Then follow the passage of Scripture slowly and see if one particular word or line strikes you more than the others. The Scripture is intended to help you enter the story of the Magi more personally. It can help to repeat a phrase from Scripture several times, slowly and reverently. Gradually you may find yourself able

to rest quietly in the words or in some aspect of the
Magi story that seems important for you.

After the Scripture stage, there are reflection
points on the Magi, each offering a different perspective on the story and a different entry into prayer.
As always, ponder these reflections carefully but with
the idea of finding one or two points that cause you
to pause and pray. You can always come back to other
aspects another time.

Session 1: The Path of Desire
Invitation
As you begin this time of reflection, close your eyes
for a few moments to allow the inner self to find
some quiet. You are here to receive some new light on
your life. Ask for the ability to get in touch with your
deeper desires. Then, perhaps say this prayer: "Lord
Jesus, you said that you are the light of the world and
our way, truth, and life. Grant that I discover how to
journey with you in this Advent time toward newness
of light, toward you."

Stillness Exercise
• As you begin this time of prayer today, pay attention to whatever sounds you can hear around you.
  Whatever your surroundings are just now, notice
  the different sounds, and notice, too, where they
  come from.

- Now allow those sounds to fade into the background as you let your attention move inward. Find a quiet place within yourself, and for a moment or two simply rest there, in the quiet at the center of yourself. Listen for God's word now, as you read from Matthew's Gospel about wise men from the East.

Scripture
Matthew 2:1–2

In the time of King Herod, after Jesus was born in Bethlehem of Judea, wise men from the East came to Jerusalem, asking, "Where is the child who has been born king of the Jews? For we observed his star at its rising, and have come to pay him homage."

Reflect

- In the second chapter of Matthew's Gospel, we are told that the wise men had "seen his star in the East and had come to worship" a newborn king. Therefore their journey began with a moment of wonder. They may have been astronomers or astrologists, who saw plenty of stars, but this one seemed different.

- What star, so to speak, stirs your desire this year? What new light invites you out of yourself? Our Advent journey of prayer is one way of being faithful to the light that calls us. In fact, this story begins with a call, a light from beyond ourselves. First, we need to pause and recognize that light. Then we need courage to let it awaken our desire. Finally, that desire may lead to movement, a movement of fidelity to the light.

• The interaction among light and desire and movement is central to the Magi story and also for our faith and our prayer. Try to make this concrete in your own situation now. Can you recognize and name the light that seems to beckon you? Can you get in touch with your deepest desire in this moment of your life? What movement or inner direction does this Advent season suggest to you? In the Gospel, the Magi story tells of a movement toward the discovery of Christ, a journey of fidelity to the light, marked also by times of darkness and danger.

Talk to God

• Saint Ignatius was surprisingly insistent that toward the beginning of a period of prayer, one should ask for a definite grace. So, journeying through this retreat, what are we seeking? Perhaps it could be in the words of Saint Ignatius to ask for inner knowledge of the Lord so that you may know and follow him. To trust that the Lord calls us to search for him this Advent and that his promise can become true for you during this time of reflection.

- Perhaps something has struck you particularly, and this is an excellent starting point for reflection. Stay with it and make it personal, but don't forget to put yourself first of all in the presence of God. Take your time; there is no hurry. Notice what hope or desire moves you.

Session 2: We Do Not Travel Alone
Invitation

As you begin this time of reflection, close your eyes for a few moments to allow the inner self to find some quiet. You are here to receive some new light on your life. Ask for the ability to get in touch with your deeper desires. Then, perhaps say this prayer: "Lord Jesus, you said that you are the light of the world and our way, truth, and life. Grant that I discover how to journey with you in this Advent time toward newness of light, toward you."

Stillness Exercise

- Begin today's prayer by focusing on your own breathing. Don't try to change its rhythm or depth; simply notice it. Be aware of the air being drawn into your lungs, and then be aware of it returning to the atmosphere.

- Now, as you breathe in, let your attention follow your breath into your chest. In Hebrew, the words for *breath* and *spirit*, as in the *Holy Spirit*, are the same. So imagine breathing in God's breath, God's Spirit, and letting the center of yourself become flooded with the Spirit's warmth and light.

- Now move your focus from your own breathing to the Spirit resting at the heart of you, in that place of stillness. From that still point, listen to God's word from Matthew's Gospel.

Scripture
Matthew 2:7–9

Then Herod secretly called for the wise men and learned from them the exact time when the star had appeared. Then he sent them to Bethlehem, saying, "Go and search diligently for the child; and when you have found him, bring me word so that I may also go and pay him homage." When they had heard the king, they set out; and there, ahead of them, went the star that they had seen at its rising, until it stopped over the place where the child was.

Reflect

- It may be helpful to reflect on the many people who have crossed our path in life and especially those who have walked with us in our faith journey. The seventeenth-century Spanish Jesuit Baltasar Gracian wrote that "life without friends is like life on a desert island," adding that to find and keep even one deep friendship in life is the greatest of blessings. Of course, many contacts with people do not become friendships, but these also influence the tone of our lives as Christians. How do I react to the stranger, the beggar, the difficult person? "Just as you did it to one of the least of these," says Jesus, "you did it to me."

- It is through the quality of our relationships that we grow and change. It is here that the heart learns generosity or else can get hurt. It is here, we hope, that our Magi-like journey toward God finds human nourishment. If we experience understanding and acceptance in friendships, we are more open to believing in the acceptance of a loving God. Just as the Magi traveled in companionship, so do we. Our prayer in preparation for Christmas can start from this aspect of our lives, and it can unfold in three moments; as an exercise in memory, in healing, and in gratitude. In each of these dimensions you can reread your story prayerfully, seeking to recognize God at work in our many human situations through the years.

Talk to God

- *Memory.* Think of parents and family, of childhood or school friends, of special relationships of trust and of love, of relationships that last and of those that were lost in the course of time. Who are the key people without whom your life would be totally different? Do this slowly. Pause on the memories that seem strong for you. Did these encounters help you become more faithful to the light that you follow (as with the Magi on their journey)? Or did some of them leave you wounded or even embittered? Remember to revisit the past (and the present) with the Lord, not just as a self-exploration.

- *Healing.* If you run into painful memories, do not avoid them. To find some healing is an important part of this pilgrimage toward Christmas. "Forgive us as we forgive": that phrase in the Our Father is stressed often in the gospel. We are told to pray for our "enemies." But that is not easy. We cannot always command our feelings, but we can try to avoid clinging to bitterness. Here is an image that could help. Think of a magnifying glass: it enlarges some words that are on the page, but it distorts the rest of the page. If some relationship has gone sour or worse, it is easy to develop a negative magnifying glass, in the sense of concentrating on resentment and forgetting to read the whole page of one's story. To break that glass is a grace, one that sets the heart free for the journey of faith. Have the courage to stay and seek that freedom from the Lord.

- *Gratitude.* In our journey with others, we hope that most of our memories will be life-giving and therefore sources of wonder and thanksgiving. We need others to set us free for love, and they do this in many different ways. Recall times of special intimacy or of ordinary enjoyment spent with others. Remember how a first casual meeting blossomed into a lasting friendship. In both our human belonging and in our relationship with the Lord, we cross thresholds into new depths. Offer thanks for the blessing of these contacts and how they have made you more open to God.

Session 3: Danger on the Road
Invitation
As you begin this time of reflection, close your eyes for a few moments to allow the inner self to find some quiet. You are here to receive some new light on your life. Ask for the ability to get in touch with your deeper desires. Then, perhaps say this prayer: "Lord Jesus, you said that you are the light of the world and our way, truth, and life. Grant that I discover how to

journey with you in this Advent time toward newness of light, toward you."

Stillness Exercise

- The prayer of each session of this retreat invites you to a different way of growing more still, more focused, in preparation for hearing God's word. Today you could begin by picking up some kind of physical object, something that you can hold easily—a cup, piece of fruit, feather, or small stone. If there is nothing at hand, you might focus on a piece of clothing you are wearing. Choose something, and sit quietly for a moment with it.

- Now turn this object over in your hands. Look closely at it. Notice how it feels, how heavy it is, whether it is rough or smooth, hard or soft. Let your whole attention, for a few moments, be focused on this object that you're holding.

- Bring your sense of touch to the reading today, as Matthew tells the story of the wise men and Herod. Imagine the stone and marble of Herod's palace, the dust of the streets, the countryside that stretches between Jerusalem and Bethlehem. Also the feel of the air, the heat or cold of the day, and the feelings of tension in Herod, the chief priests, and the wise men.

Scripture

Matthew 2:1–8

In the time of King Herod, after Jesus was born in Bethlehem of Judea, wise men from the East came to Jerusalem, asking, "Where is the child who has been born king of the Jews? For we observed his star at its rising, and have come to pay him homage." When King Herod heard this, he was frightened, and all Jerusalem with him; and calling together all the chief priests and scribes of the people, he inquired of them where the Messiah was to be born. They told him, "In Bethlehem of Judea; for so it has been written by the prophet:

> And you, Bethlehem, in the land of Judah,
> are by no means least among the rulers of Judah;
> for from you shall come a ruler
> who is to shepherd my people Israel."

Then Herod secretly called for the wise men and learned from them the exact time when the star had appeared. Then he sent them to Bethlehem, saying, "Go and search diligently for the child; and when you have found him, bring me word so that I may also go and pay him homage."

Reflect

- If the Magi were being guided by a star, why did they consult people in Jerusalem and end up being interrogated by Herod? Although the Gospel text does not say it explicitly, it seems that the star disappeared from view. What we are told is that when they left Jerusalem, the star appeared again and gave them "great joy." This is a fascinating and often overlooked detail. It also suggests a pendulum of spiritual moods, a contrast that Saint Ignatius considered central for discernment, the difference between "desolation" and "consolation."

- Everyone has experienced this in his or her own way. There are times when everything is going well, when you are in tune with the good spirit and can move forward in faith and hope and love. In other words, you are like the Magi when they are confidently guided by the star. But there are other times when the light seems blocked, when you find yourself confused or troubled, and when instead of gently moving forward you can become paralyzed and lost. This is a situation of spiritual danger, when deception can easily lead us astray. The invitation here is to recognize this contrast of spirits in your own life and in your times of prayer. The Magi set out on their journey in consolation, and that consolation returned after a time of absence. But in this story, Jerusalem sums up another spirit, and they nearly fell into the trap that Herod set for them.

- Notice that the Gospel text speaks about Herod and the whole city being troubled or disturbed by the question of the Magi as to where Jesus was born. But the Magi are asking the wrong people. In Jerusalem they find themselves without their star and surrounded by a world of power, envy, and violence. Later on in the story, the Magi will be warned in a dream not to return to Herod. Without this special message, they could easily have reported back to the murderous Herod. Remember that Saint Ignatius offers a classic piece of wisdom: never make a decision when you are in desolation.

Talk to God

- We are more vulnerable when we are not in touch with the light of the good spirit. What do you consider your danger points to be? What are your usual sources of strength or consolation? This whole journey of faith, symbolized by the Magi story, reminds us that the life of faith runs into difficulty sometimes. So it is healthy to recognize these moments of weakness and important to pray when we experience periods of desolation—as when the star seems to disappear.

- The religious intellectuals of Jerusalem consult their books and give Herod the right answer about the birthplace of the Messiah: Bethlehem of Judea. Saint Augustine commented ironically on these experts: they liked offering other people directions but would not undertake any quest themselves. They remained stuck, and their impersonal knowledge was fruitless in them. Once again, this is a form of desolation or non-movement, whereas consolation is characterized by growth and the courage to change.

- It is also possible to widen our horizon and to read this Gospel tale of two cities in the light of today's divided world. Herod and Jerusalem can stand for the closed selfishness of the powerful, those who directly or indirectly oppress the poor of our planet. But Bethlehem, as we will see, stands for another attitude of life, a simplicity that is open to adoration.

Session 4: Lost in Wonder

Invitation

As you begin this time of reflection, close your eyes for a few moments to allow the inner self to find some quiet. You are here to receive some new light on your life. Ask for the ability to get in touch with your deeper desires. Then, perhaps say this prayer: "Lord Jesus, you said that you are the light of the world and our way, truth, and life. Grant that I discover how to journey with you in this Advent time toward newness of light, toward you."

Stillness Exercise

- Today, light a candle or choose an icon or other sacred image. Focus your gaze on it for a minute or two, until you feel yourself grow still.

- Allow aspects of this candle flame or image to soak into your thoughts. Pay attention to the colors of the flame or the picture and how those colors make you feel. Notice the shapes that emerge— circles or ovals, lines, textures.

- Bring this attention, now, to the story of the wise men following the singular image: a star.

Scripture
Matthew 2:9–11a

When they had heard the king, they set out; and there, ahead of them, went the star that they had seen at its rising, until it stopped over the place where the child was. When they saw that the star had stopped, they were overwhelmed with joy. On entering the house, they saw the child with Mary his mother; and they knelt down and paid him homage.

Reflect

- We come now to the climax of the journey of the Magi, to the moment they find Jesus and worship him. They have traveled the short distance of a few miles from Jerusalem to Bethlehem. For them, Jerusalem had been a place of disturbance and even of desolation and inner darkness. But the light of the star returned to guide them to the small town of Bethlehem, stopping over the house where they discover Mary and Jesus. Notice again that this stage of the journey is marked by "great joy." If Herod's Jerusalem was a city of power and intrigue, Bethlehem proves to be a place of simplicity and prayer. These two places represent spiritual spaces, not just geographical locations.

- Something extraordinary is happening here. If we imagine the Magi realizing that this child is in some way divine, then everything changes for them. Their journey from the East is now met by another journey of God into this world. The searchers now find themselves sought for by this child. Here is a moment for pausing in prayer, asking to realize that all your desire to encounter Christ is embraced and transformed by his desire to come toward you.

Talk to God

- Perhaps the Magi also had to cross this surprising threshold into adoration. What is adoration? It is the highest form of prayer, in which someone is overwhelmed by a sense of the glory and presence of God. In the Bible it is associated with intense awareness of both the holiness and the closeness of God.

- In the case of the Magi, the divine presence was hidden in a helpless child. They were graced, it seems, with being able to recognize the extraordinary in the ordinary and to enter a wordless space of contemplation. We are therefore moved at this time toward a prayer of quiet. It is worth remembering that bodily position can be important as an expression of reverence. It may also help to repeat some phrase as one imagines oneself there in the Gospel scene: "Lord Jesus" or "Hallowed be thy name" or (addressed to Mary) "The Lord is with thee." But do not forget to let the words quiet into a silence where the heart, "lost in wonder," enjoys the presence of Jesus.

- In the Spiritual Exercises of Saint Ignatius, he insists that God seeks to communicate directly with the retreatant, "inflaming the soul with his love," and that the director should not get in the way of this "immediate" presence of God. This is the space of adoration and indeed of transformation, and it is open to everyone in his or her own way. It invites us into a quiet reverence beyond "their many words," as Jesus himself said (Matthew 6:8). The theologian Hans Urs von Balthasar said, "Contemplation starts when the mystery begins to reveal itself in all its vastness . . . something impossible has happened: God manifests himself in a human life." As you reflect at this time, have the courage to simplify the gaze of your heart before this epiphany, this glory that is both veiled and unveiled.

Session 5: Carrying a Gift
Invitation
As you begin this time of reflection, close your eyes for a few moments to allow the inner self to find some quiet. You are here to receive some new light on your life. Ask for the ability to get in touch with your deeper desires. Then, perhaps say this prayer: "Lord Jesus, you said that you are the light of the world and our way, truth, and life. Grant that I discover how to journey with you in this Advent time toward newness of light, toward you."

Stillness Exercise

- Today, choose a simple phrase to help you focus and become quiet. Use "Come, Lord Jesus," "Lord, have mercy," "I welcome your peace," or something else that feels comfortable for you.

- Speak this phrase aloud, repeatedly, for a minute or two. Allow the sound and rhythm of the words to shift your attention away from other distractions. Then whisper the phrase repeatedly as your whole body becomes more still and settled.

- Then, think the phrase repeatedly for a few moments before allowing the words to cease and your interior quiet to begin. From this place, hear what Matthew's Gospel has to say today.

Scripture

Matthew 2:10–11

When they saw that the star had stopped, they were overwhelmed with joy. On entering the house, they saw the child with Mary his mother; and they knelt down and paid him homage. Then, opening their treasure-chests, they offered him gifts of gold, frank-incense, and myrrh.

Reflect

- Of course the custom of Christmas gifts has its origin here, and even though we rightly complain about this religious feast becoming so commercialized, we can hope that a spirit of generosity survives the consumerism. But there are deeper dimensions here upon which to meditate. Each of the Magi brought a different gift. What do you do with what life has given you? How do you live your freedom? What is the unique gift you have received and that only you can bring to this world? God made each one of us different. Nobody else, in the whole of human history, has the same personality and situation that you have. Your call is yours and yours alone. And your call is to live your particular gift in your particular life setting.

- Other moments of Scripture also invite us to pray about our gifts and to find the courage to live them. Think of the parable of the talents, which is an invitation to live our freedom creatively, embracing our opportunities to grow and to give. In this same parable we find someone who buries his one talent out of fear and who is strongly rebuked for wasting even the limited gift received. The invitation here is to wake up to our possibilities for giving, in spite of the inevitable limitations of each life.

- The Magi "opened their treasures." Perhaps we can also recall the parable of Jesus that speaks of finding a hidden treasure (Matthew 13:44). While the third person in the parable of the talents buries his or her talent out of fear, the one who discovers treasure hidden in a field buries it again but in the spirit of joy and anticipation of owning that field. Here we have a contrast between two attitudes to the challenge of our freedom: fear or gratitude— paralyzing anxiety or energizing trust. You might like to pause and reflect prayerfully on your typical responses, recognizing more the gifts you have than those you lack.

Talk to God

- As we journey on in life, most of us become aware of decline and passivity. Some of the old gifts are less present, especially those that depend on energy and good health. But as we get older, perhaps new gifts are born, such as a more relaxed enjoyment of people or a new kind of wisdom. In spite of, or even because of, our limitations, our gifts can find a new ease and simplicity. In fact, artists' presentations of the Magi usually show an old one with white hair, side by side with a young and energetic one and a third from another culture or race.

- As Saint Paul says, in essence, when he writes to the Ephesians: "You are God's work of art, created in Christ Jesus to live the good life" (Ephesians 2:10). In other words, God is shaping us all the time for

goodness and beauty. To reflect on your gifted-
ness, you could adapt this famous prayer of Saint
Ignatius: "Take and Receive": "You have given
me all my gifts. To You I offer them all. Bless my
living of them with your love and grace. That is
enough for me."

- A final dimension in praying our gifts is to remember the big scene of the world and its many
struggles and needs. Any act of goodness, however small, is a source of transformation. When we
pray "Thy kingdom come," we are asking that our
efforts be part of God's great action of saving the
world from evil. If all were to live their God-given
gifts, our planet would be a different place.

Session 6: Another Way of Life

Invitation

As you begin this time of reflection, close your eyes
for a few moments to allow the inner self to find
some quiet. You are here to receive some new light on
your life. Ask for the ability to get in touch with your
deeper desires. Then, perhaps say this prayer: "Lord
Jesus, you said that you are the light of the world and
our way, truth, and life. Grant that I discover how to
journey with you in this Advent time toward newness
of light, toward you."

Stillness Exercise

As we've made our way through the different sessions of this retreat, you will have drawn on the exercises of paying attention to sounds and textures, to your breath, to an image, an object, and a phrase—all for the purpose of growing quiet and focused. If one of these practices has been especially helpful, take a few moments now to go through that exercise. Don't worry if you can't remember the details of how it was presented here; just let your sense of how things work lead you deeper into stillness and silence. When you feel ready, give your attention to this passage from Matthew's Gospel.

Scripture
Matthew 2:11–12

On entering the house, they saw the child with Mary his mother; and they knelt down and paid him homage. Then, opening their treasure chests, they offered him gifts of gold, frankincense, and myrrh. And having been warned in a dream not to return to Herod, they left for their own country by another road.

Reflect

• The Magi story ends with a change of direction: they are warned in a dream not to return to Herod and to depart to their own country by another way.

In light of this we can reflect on two concluding themes for our retreat: God rescues us from evil, and discovering Christ means living differently.

- The last line of the Our Father—"Deliver us from evil"—implies that we often need God's guidance and protection. If the star spoke to the Magi from outside, the dream spoke from inside. Although it is not explicit in Matthew's text, this dream indicates how the Spirit acts in our lives. Jesus at the Last Supper promised to send another Paraclete (literally, defense advocate) to be our defender in the trials and complexities of life. Even after their encounter with the child Jesus, the Magi needed a deeper grace to save them from evil, from Herod who had appeared trustworthy. What are some of the attractive but deceptive surfaces that you need to see through today? Give thanks for times when you have been saved from danger.

- Faith involves a battleground. The "world" in John's Gospel is loved by God so much that God sends his Son, but the "world" is also a negative word, a place of resistance to, and refusal of, God. Therefore faith needs to be countercultural, not in the sense of being hostile to everything modern but rather alert to the darkness around us. Try to make this personal, prayerfully identifying some of the attractive but shallow tendencies you see around you that can undermine the quality of your Christian life.

Talk to God

- Being a Christian means being changed by the encounter with Christ and often choosing to resist the dominant lifestyle. In his encyclical *Laudato Si*, Pope Francis focuses on this challenge of how we see ourselves in this world. If we humans forget faith and put ourselves at the center, then what is convenient becomes acceptable and "all else becomes relative." A vision rooted in Christ asks us to "look at reality in a different way"—or, as the Magi text puts it, to go by "another road." In this spirit we are encouraged to live "a lifestyle and spirituality" that could "generate resistance" to many of the superficial assumptions of today's culture.

- What are the foundations of Christ's new kingdom? Surely the most challenging summary of his overthrow of worldly values comes in the Beatitudes. Here we have perhaps an autobiographical account of Jesus' heart. You can ponder them slowly as invitations to a daily conversion of your own heart. But be careful not to fall into the trap of making them too otherworldly. Surprisingly, they are true even in this life. Surely it is happier to be gentle rather than aggressive, to forgive rather than resent, to nourish peace rather than hostility.